My Grandma Could do ANYTHING at the BEACH

by Ric Dilz

For all the Grandmas who bring sunshine to the beach!

REINdesigns, inc.

Boulder, Colorado

Illustration & Design by: Nancy Maysmith, Helen H. Harrison & Ric Dilz

P9-DCI-497

My Grandma
doesn't bungee jump
from a helicopter...

But she could!

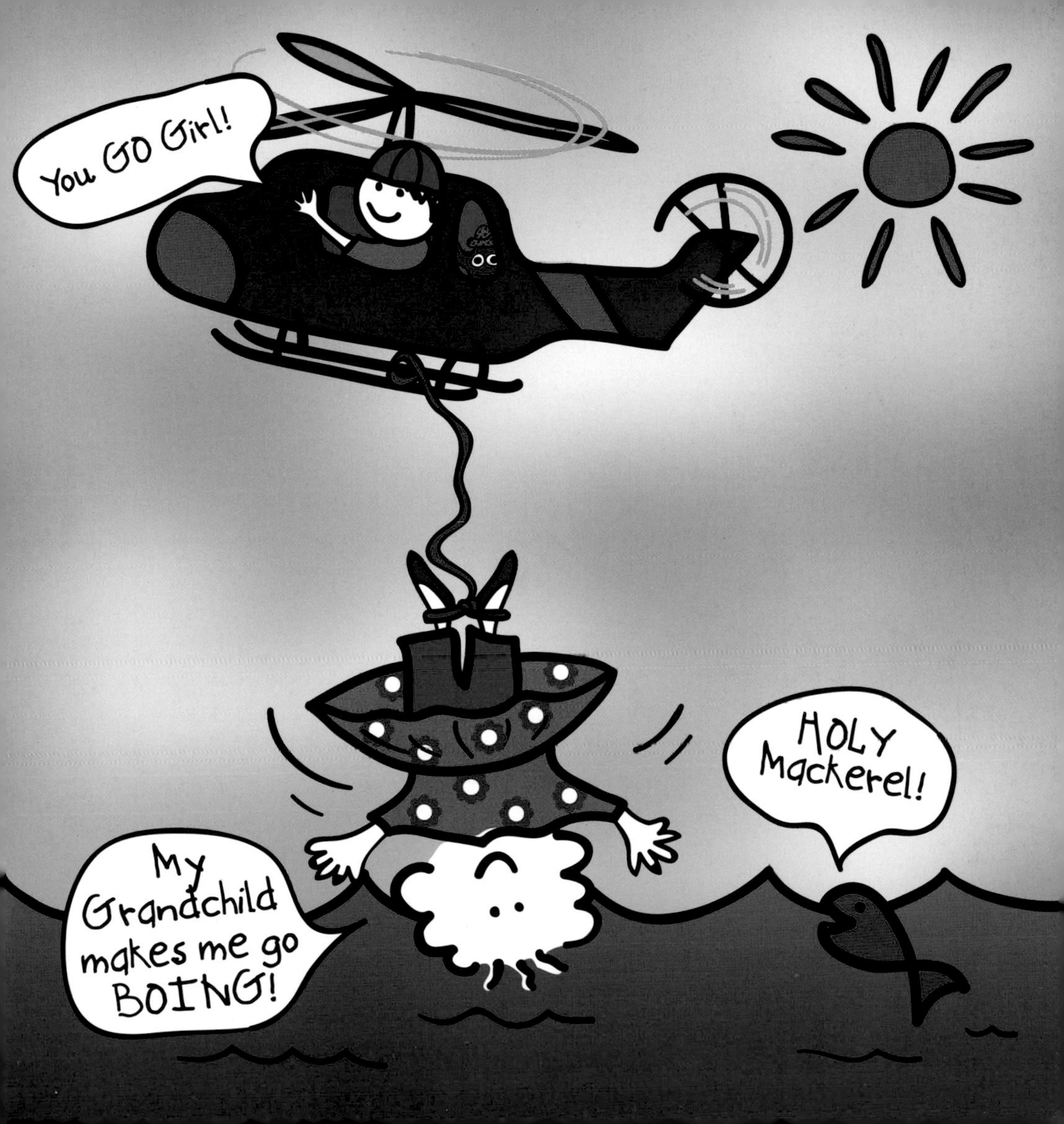
You GO Girl!
HOLY Mackerel!
My Grandchild makes me go BOING!

My Grandma
doesn't do tricks
on water skis...

But she could!

My Grandma
doesn't jump on
a water trampoline...

But she could!

My Grandma
doesn't hang glide
over the beach...

But she could!

My Grandma
doesn't body surf
a 20 foot wave...

But she could!

My Grandma
doesn't
catch monster fish...

But she could!

My Grandma
doesn't jet ski
huge waves...

But she could!

My Grandma
doesn't do tricks
on a paddleboard...

But she could!

My Grandma
doesn't build
giant sandcastles...

But she could!

My Grandma
doesn't windsurf wildly
with a goldfish...

But she could!

My Grandma
doesn't juggle
ice cream cones...

But she could!

My Grandma
doesn't rock out
on a guitar
around a campfire...

But she could!

My Grandma
could do lots of things,
but I'm so happy with
the one thing she does
the best...

Can you find these things in the book?

Beach Tongue Twisters

Frannie's fancy flip flops.

Can you say "Fancy flops three times real fast?
Fancy Flops! Fancy Flops! Fancy Flops!

Petey the parrot picks pickles.

Can you say Picky Petey three times real fast?
Picky Petey! Picky Petey! Picky Petey!

Frogs find funky friends funny.

Can you say Funky Friends three times real fast?
Funky Friends! Funky Friends! Funky Friends!

Crabby crabs crumble cookies.

Can you say crumble cookie three times real fast?
Crumble Cookie! Crumble Cookie! Crumble Cookie!

Did you find me, Starry, in every picture?

Share more laughs with these fun books!

Available at www.jibberjabbers.com/books

Published by Rein Designs, Inc. Boulder, Colorado

ISBN: 978-0-9859684-1-0

Library of Congress Control Number: 2014903592

Printed in China